THE LIONESS

It's time to ROAR
(Rejoice, Overcome, Arise, Recover)

ELECT LADY DONNA BEARD

THE LIONESS: It's Time to ROAR

Copyright© 2018 by Elect Lady Donna Beard.

All rights reserved.

Elect Lady Donna Beard
P.O. BOX 932
Petal, MS 39465
601-564-WOPM
www.wopwithelectladybeard.com

No part of this book may be reproduced, stored in a retrieval system, or transmitted in any form or by any means, electronic, mechanical, photocopying, recording, scanning, or otherwise, without the prior written permission of the Author.

Scripture quotations marked NIV are taken from THE HOLY BIBLE, NEW INTERNATIONAL VERSION®, NIV® Copyright © 1973, 1978, 1984, 2011 by Biblica, Inc.® Used by permission. All rights reserved worldwide.

Scripture quotations are from The ESV® Bible (The Holy Bible, English Standard Version®), copyright © 2001 by Crossway, a publishing ministry of Good News Publishers. Used by permission. All rights reserved.

Scripture quotations taken from the New American Standard Bible® (NASB), Copyright © 1960, 1962, 1963, 1968, 1971, 1972, 1973, 1975, 1977, 1995 by The Lockman Foundation. Used by permission. www.Lockman.org

Cover Art: JP Designsart
www.jpdesignsart.com

**Interior Design | Author Support:
DHBonner Virtual Solutions, LLC**
www.dhbonner.net

ISBN: 978-0-692-13734-5

Printed in the United States of America

Table of Contents

Foreword iii
Her-Story 1
Growing Pains 11
Could I Get a Glimpse? 19
Living in Silence 27
Devasted, But Not Destroyed! 35
He Assured Me 43
My Next Chapter 47
Roaring in Anguish 55
The Lioness Den 59
R.O.A.R. (Rejoice. Overcome. Arise. Recover.) 63
The Lioness 69
About the Author 73

God Never Ends a Story,

Without Bringing Back *the Glory!*

This book is dedicated to my Mom, Dorothy J. Bolton...
you are the epitome of strength, faith, love, and sacrifice; thank you for all those prayers that were in
reserve for your children.

To my siblings James Cherry, Lobie Bolton, Lacteria "Michelle" Bolton and Sheryl "Elaine" Bradley... thank you for support
during the writing of this memoir.
I pray this book provokes you to live life
to the fullest and on purpose.

Acknowledgments

First and foremost, I want to thank my Lord and Savior Jesus Christ. You had the Master Plan for my life, and I believe it could not be reversed. I'm still a dependent, and I cannot do anything without you.

And, to my Amazing husband, Apostle Paul Beard, thank you for being my teacher, covering, and my greatest cheerleader.

To my children and their families, Paul Beard Jr. (Betty), you guys were my first editors. Thanks for the countless hours critiquing my work; Cordaryl who became the chef during those times, and Shamaiah (Robert) for listening and supporting this project. Momma loves you all to life!

To my spiritual family, *Dominion and Power Family Life Center International*, for the many years of support and love. We have grown together, and I love you guys forever.

And to Minister Sinyon Reed when I called you answered, thank you for your strong gifting of writing and counsel.

A special thanks to one of my spiritual sons, Min. Matthew Naylor, for always encouraging me to write the book. It came to pass!

To the JP Designsarts Team, thank you for your patience, creativity, and witty inventions, I was your assignment.

Last, but not least, to my publisher, Elder Desireé Harris-Bonner, for your patience, kindness, and long-suffering during the process of perfecting this vision.

To God be the Glory!

Foreword

Wow! How do I begin to talk about this author? She's my wife of thirty-three years, my friend of thirty-seven years, and the mother of our three beautiful children.

She's amazing and embodies poise as she gracefully moves about the Body of Christ. In this season, she has been moved to invite you, the readers, into her world, in which she gained a testimony that has catapulted her into her place in both Ministry and Life. I believe as you read this powerful and compelling script, which details her life, you will come away informed, inspired, and encouraged.

Informed, because you never know what God allows a person to go through to get to their place in Him. *Inspired*, because of the strength and tenacity with which the author had to have. *Encouraged*, because you will be assured to know that in whatever you have gone through, or are currently going through, God is going to bring you out and get the Glory out of your Story.

Apostle Paul L. Beard Sr.; Founder/Overseer
Dominion and Power Family Life Center, International

Her-Story

"There is no greater agony than bearing an untold story inside of you."

~ Maya Angelou

My father had gotten into some trouble.

He decided to leave the city and go on the run, he changed his name, acquired a new identity, and abandoned my mother; leaving her to raise two small children alone.

Being that I was only a toddler when this happened and way too young to know the full story of his disappearance, I honestly cannot even remember what he looked like. In that day and time, if something bad occurred in the family, no one spoke of it. We were taught *"what goes on in this house, stays in this house."*

Even today, as I drive through the old neighborhood, there is such a strong spirit of darkness that hovers over that city, I think to myself, what secrets do you yet hold? Who am I? Are there other parts of my story that are yet unknown to me?

Nevertheless, there we were. My mother, married, yet a single parent, and living with the uncertainty of when, *or if*, her husband would ever return.

From the little that she shared with me, her life had not been easy, even as a young lady. In those days, being a light complexioned black girl was difficult. I could imagine that things were tough for her; yet as the days, and then years, passed and Dad did not show up, she had no choice but to simply take strength and move on.

Life continued.

After some time, Mom met this tall, dark, and handsome young man. Let's just call him Mr. John. Well, common law marriages were normal back then, and due to the unknown whereabouts of my Father, she could not get a divorce. I can still remember me and my younger brother, Anthony, crying as we found ourselves relocating about thirty minutes away from our grandparents and everyone we knew, to move in with him… our new stepdad.

Mr. John lived with his mother; everyone called her "Momma Mae." Well, next door to Momma Mae was a little white house, with music coming out of it. The music was loud every night; especially on the weekends when the locals would come and dance, drink alcohol, and at times, fights broke out.

Mom would sometimes go because Mr. John wanted her to be with him. Now and then she would drink a little, as well. I knew this was not my mother's character, but she just did it to keep him happy. I would cry when I saw her doing that, because

THE LIONESS

Mr. John drank, and when he drank, he turned into something else. And, one scary person was enough.

Anthony and I would stay locked up in the house; depending on each other.

Over time, we began to understand that Momma Mae was the owner of the club, and we hated it. I was so afraid of that place and those people. It was incredibly terrifying how much people's personalities would change. The smoking, cursing, fighting, drunkenness, and guns, through the eyes of a child, was frightening.

Monday would come, and life would be much quieter. Our new stepdad and many of the others would have to go to work. It was business as usual, with a few patrons coming by to buy a drink and hang around a little. But, by Thursday night, the noise level grew, and it was back to the weekend; which they lived for.

Mr. John would leave his mom's house to spend time at her business, as a quiet, mysterious man. Later, he would come back staggering, talking loud, and his eyes blood-shot red. Intoxicated, he was vicious and evil. It was as if he were an entirely different person.

We were engulfed in so much fear that in order for things to be somewhat okay, Mom had to drink with him. Otherwise, he would get into a rage. The cursing would be foul and filled with such anger, that only his elder sister, Auntie Ree, could calm him down. We were always walking on pins and needles, tiptoeing around him so that we wouldn't tick him off. So, whenever he would begin to become irate, we'd either take off running to try and find Auntie Ree or we would hide; she was the only one that could calm him down.

At times, we would hear our Mom in the other room screaming, but she would not let us come in the room because he had begun physically and verbally abusing her. Many days, she would try not to make noise and just take whatever he was doing to her, so that we would not become alarmed or get hurt. We had no idea what was going on behind that closed door. *Was he choking her? Was he sodomizing her? Was he torturing her?*

Jesus!!! We are too small to help, all we could do was to beg him not to hurt her. One thing he did not do, however, was put scars on her face. There would be bruises under her clothing, but never on her face.

In the small town where we lived, there was a little opening in the woods that we would walk through to visit our neighbors; all of whom were related to our stepdad. Some days, we would run there trying to get help for our mom. Even though most of them knew what was happening, they would not get involved. And, by the time he would have beaten her, choked her, or only God knows what else to her, he would run into the house to grab his gun. This gave Mom some time to run and hide.

Occasionally, Momma Mae would get onto him. One time, Momma Mae even hit him over the head with a beer bottle; breaking it over his head. So, sometimes she would be of help… and sometimes she wouldn't. But, for the most part, she did try to come to our rescue. We had a love for Momma Mae, even though we were not her biological grandchildren.

She did not mistreat us, and even to this day, I have fond memories of her.

Mom tried to help anybody, and she lived to please him. She was more of the breadwinner than he was. He would get paid on

THE LIONESS

Friday and be broke by Sunday. Yet, he still expected Mom to have his food cooked and brought to him, and the lights better not be cut off. However, her paycheck could only go so far. She was unable to get food stamps because, together, their incomes were too high. So, she struggled to feed and clothe us, while he always wanted his full course meal.

I remember one particular day he had been drinking, and some of the locals had lied on my mom; saying she had done something or other. For whatever reason, he lit into her, accusing her of what he had been told.

At over six feet tall, Mr. John loved his guns and his knives; always having one or the other or both on him. So, after hanging out with the guys, he came home from the club, of course in a rage, and started beating on my Mom. The men were just standing around, no one trying to help. So, while I am screaming, Anthony (about six or seven at this time) tries to stop him.

Our stepdad picked Anthony up by the collar and threw him down. Seeing this, Mom tried to help and run at the same time, and Mr. John grabbed the pistol from behind his back and pointed it at my Mom. From the crowd, one of the men, Mr. Lee, came and snatched the gun from him and ran through that little opening in the woods; saving my mother's life.

To this day, this man could never imagine the respect that I have for him, as I see him aging gracefully. From that moment he was, and yet is, my hero.

We were able to live and have our mom another day.
My stepdad woke up the next morning, saying he did not remember any of that; crying and apologizing, and telling my mom that he loves her and wouldn't do that again.

Mom always made us go to church and Sunday school; even when she did not go. And, if she went to church, Mr. John would just accuse her of sleeping with the preachers or the deacons.

Jealousy was the rage of this man.

***

One thing about a small town, everybody knows what's going on in your family. We were so ashamed and embarrassed to go to school, church, etc., as we were the talk of the town.

It is incredible how cruel kids can be; making fun of us, picking at us, and calling us names. I think this is why I was so shy and quiet. I had a lot of shame, inward pain, and fear. And, no one could even conceive of the environment that we were living in. Anthony and I were afraid to tell anybody the truth of it all, so I just turned all that I was going through inwardly.

This began to not only take a toll on my mind, but my physical body also had started to show symptoms of wearing down under the situation. I had developed a nervous condition, and whenever I became scared or nervous, I would have bad stomachaches.

I can remember Mom taking me to the hospital, in an effort to discover exactly was going on with me; however, the doctors could not tell what was causing my nervousness. But, if I shared with them what was going on, they may take my brother and me away from our mom.

Some of the parents in the neighborhood had their kids taken from them if they were considered unfit or negligent. And then, they would have to fight to get them back. Our environment was hostile, and we thought this could probably happen to us.

Many nights, my mom was so severely hurt, that I thought if she went to be with this Jesus they were teaching us to pray to in Sunday school, she would not have to continue to suffer like this. The abuse was torture. But then, what would happen to Anthony and me?!

During this time, Anthony and I shared a bed. And, if anybody knows country people, you could hear cars coming from a mile away, and by the sound of each car, you knew exactly who the owner of the car was. My nerves were so shot that I would hear Mr. John's vehicle coming down the road and my body would begin to shake so much that it would wake my brother up out of his sleep. The two of us would get close to one another; hoping that he would just stagger in and go to sleep, instead of messing with anyone.

It was bad.

Eventually, the club closed down, we moved out of his mother's house, and the club became our new home. At least we were still close to Momma Mae in case something happened, or she was sober enough to stop him. Still, Mr. John ran around with the guys from the neighborhood; most of them related and meant him no good. Some were jealous of him and mom. He was a very handsome man, and mom was absolutely beautiful.

It seemed they would always put him up to do stuff; like the guys would start fights with other guys at other clubs, neighboring cities, etc., and he was right there with them. Perhaps it was because he needed to feel as if he belonged.

Nevertheless, they all did what we called in that day, went for bad!

On the outside, they saw him as a hero; publicly he would help anybody. It was as if they were the family and we were his enemies. He chose them over and over again.

Now, I'm from the time of wood-burning heaters and having to go pump water. So, one night, we were at home with Momma Mae, sitting around the heater and trying to stay warm, and one of the guys came and told Mom and Momma Mae that our stepdad had gotten shot by some of the neighboring guys. He said it was critical, and that Mr. John wanted his mom.

I hate to say that as I write this, a part of my brother and me hoped he would not make it. Our feeling was indifferent; I feel so ashamed, even as I remember. But, it was either him or Mom or us. I thought we could now be free. At any rate, he recovered.

As time went on, Anthony and I were inseparable. We got into kid fights, but we loved each other; we were all we had. We would run, play games, climb trees; you know… the usual stuff.

Anthony was shorter than most of his peers, but he excelled in everything he did. I wanted to protect him because I was the oldest, and he needed to protect us because he was the 'man.' I felt so bad for my brother. Aside from being treated as an outcast and having to battle issues of acceptance, he also had to bear the burden of his desire to protect us girls.

Only time would tell the full impact this was going to have on him, the pain it would produce, and what was happening to him; especially since we still did not know our real dad's whereabouts or if he was ever coming back.

THE LIONESS

We missed our grandparents and were living in a constant state of fear. But, I was soon to learn more about that Jesus they taught us about in Sunday school...

The Lion of the Tribe of Judah.

Growing Pains

*"We don't grow when things are easy;
we grow when we face challenges."*

~Unknown

Soon, Mom began having more children. The first was a big, yellow, ten-pound boy that looked like his Dad; having mom's coloring and Mr. John's features.

They called him Jr.

Now, my stepdad loved some babies. So, we thought this would make a change in his life. Especially, since while she was pregnant, he would not hit her in the stomach.

Later, two more precious baby girls came along. The first girl, Micki, has beautiful, curly, black hair. And, our baby sister, Lulu, looks just like mom. Still, between the birthing of our little family, we were yet suffering. There were days when I thought that Mom would not make it. Like the day she needed to go to the store. I feared her getting into the car with him when he drank because it did not take long for him to get drunk and I had no way of knowing what would, or could, be happening to her.

At the time, we were still living in the club, and I remember he tried to run over her with his car; thankfully, only catching the heel of her boot, as she tried to get out the way. When she fell in the woods, I thought he was successful in harming her, but she was okay.

Although she wanted to protect us, I could feel her pain, though she tried to hide the tears on her face; sometimes lying to me so that I wouldn't know what was going on. By now, Mom had a nervous condition and was smoking a lot, and in secret, he had worked on her mind so fiercely that I believe a demonic spirit of fear had overtaken her.

Mr. John had a knife called a Dutch. He would tell her that if she ever left him, he would kill the whole family; and I believed that he would do it! He detailed how he'd start with her by cutting from the bottom corner of her eye and cut her face all the way up. One day, he took that Dutch and almost cut her thumb off.

She had to have stitches.

Since there were more children to protect, whenever things broke out, we had to try to get the babies and hide in the woods with them. Sometimes, we would run to Auntie Ree's, who would take us in, until he had slept it off and we would go back home.

Another time, we ran back home to our Grandparents and Great Grands, thirty miles away. As I mentioned earlier, they were taught not to get into married people's business.

THE LIONESS

So, while we could stay with them for a short period, they left Mom and Mr. John to work it out.

One night, he showed up there with his shotgun; calling her to the truck and saying, *"If you don't get them children and get your *so-and-so* back to the house, I'm going to shoot up the place."* She believed him, and to protect them, she took us and went back home.

The Police were not much help either, because they feared him, so we continued to live under those conditions; running and hiding.

Where were we to go to escape his wrath?

From time to time, the older women who lived alone would take us in and hide us until things calmed down. They were our angels; the ones we called Cousin Alnora, Cousin Julie, Aunt Lillie Mae, and Aunt Helen. They are now resting in peace, and I won't ever be able to forget them.

My stepdad was a manly man. He was one of the greatest hunters and fishermen I know. And, he could grill or cook anything. If any of you know anything about buffalo fish, *oh my*, he could filet that fish like nobody else. We all loved him in our own way. In fact, he was the only father figure we knew, so we did not hate him. But, we feared him so much.

Many times, when things would happen, Mom would admonish us not to tell him; therefore, there were lots of secrets we had amongst ourselves because we did not want to give him an excuse to hurt her.

But hurt people really do hurt other people.

Mr. John loved holidays; especially Christmas, as December was his birth month. I don't care how much he drank, and sometimes he would stay out all night drinking, but he would always come home for Christmas.

Mom used to buy him remote-controlled cars, just like the boys. He also liked to get those vintage models that he had to glue together, with the little engine in the hood. It was a source of great relaxation for him, and while it required skill, I could also see the kid in him come out; that little boy sweetness.

The five of us kids enjoyed Christmas as well. We looked forward to helping mom decorate and trim the tree. What would it be this year... evergreen with candy canes, or full of angel hair, or white all over? It didn't matter, Mom was very creative and multi-talented, and so it would be beautiful, no matter what.

On the other hand, we also feared Christmas; we thought if we got too happy, expecting to have a great time, something would happen. Things that appear to be too good usually ended up bad.

One Christmas, my stepdad was in the yard drinking with some friends and standing around a bonfire they had started with a pile of tires. Again, he was such a very jealous man, and any little thought that hit his mind would tick him off; an idle mind truly is the devil's workshop. Well, I had noticed that he was beginning to get into that dark mood, so nervously, I decided to go to him and say something like, *"How are you doing?"*

In an attempt to change his spirit, I saw evil coming upon him through his thoughts; he was getting angrier and angrier at just an idea, not an action.

Well, he hugged me, but as his hands went down my back, I felt very uncomfortable; stepping away in an attempt to calm things down. This only made him more irate. So, my brother and

I tried to run for help and make sure that our younger siblings were safe. Still, by the time we got back, we could see the tissue in mom's upper arm, hanging out (visual).

I don't know to this day how this happened; a metal bar stool went through her arm and out the other side. They were taking my Mom to the hospital to see if she needed stitches and he went with her. Regrettably, each time we ran, it left so much time in between to hurt her. The half would never be told about what she actually suffered within those timeframes.

So, later that evening, Mom went ahead and finished cooking our holiday dinner... with one arm in a sling. She was always trying to make sure we could have a good holiday; trying to make sure we would have a Christmas that appeared as normal as possible.

Life went on... as we knew it. There were some good days. And, there were some bad ones; the cycle continuing to repeat itself over and over again. Him stumbling in drunk, him cocking his 45 and pointing it at my mom's head, us screaming and begging for him not to hurt her, and then him choking her, and our collecting the children and running into the arms of one of our angels; who hid us until things calmed down.

How much more could we stand before one or all of us were eventually killed? What would be the end of this?

***

We were now living in a little two-bedroom trailer, and of course, we all slept in the same bed. Mr. John, a little drunk, was asleep on the couch, and my mom was down the hall in her room.

This particular night, Anthony was sleeping on the wall side, and I was facing the door, on the outside of the bed. The lights were off, so it was dark, and I just happened to turn over and see my stepdad stooping down by the side of the bed, about to touch me.

When I screamed, he acted as if he had just come running down the hall to check on us. At least, that's what I heard him telling my mom.

"You better come check on the kids!" All while screwing the light bulb back into the socket.

When Mom finally made it down the hall and into our bedroom, she turned on the lights and asked, *"What's wrong with you?"* With Mr. John towering above her petite, 5'2" frame, looking down at me with a facial expression that said, "You better not say nothing," I did exactly that... I said absolutely nothing.

My mom asked again, "What's wrong with you?"

I opened my mouth and said that I had a nightmare. I was so afraid that my stomach began hurting and my nerves were shot. But, I said, "I'm okay Mom."

After a few moments, she left the room and went back to bed, and he went back into the living room. Soon, I could hear him beginning to snore.

That night, I felt like I was going to die. Fear had gripped me yet again, and I could not sleep; not knowing if he was coming back or not. I was shaking so bad that I woke my siblings who were in bed with me.

THE LIONESS

So, I decided to go to my Mom's room, and tell her that I could not sleep. Thankfully, she told me to get in bed with her, putting me behind her facing the wall, where I would be out his way... just in case.

In the quiet, stillness of her room, Mom asked me again, *"What happened?"*

This time, I told her that my stepdad had been squatting down by my bed, and when I turned over and saw him, I screamed because I thought that he was going to molest me. As soon as I finished talking, Mom quickly got out of bed, went into the living room, and started screaming and trying to wake him up. But, he wouldn't.

Personally, I believe he played sleep that night. He wasn't that drunk! He was sober enough to unscrew the light bulb, in case I woke up and caught him, and before Mom had come into the room, he had screwed it back in.

Of all that he had done to my mother, I had never seen her as angry as she was in that moment. While continuing to scream at him, she began beating on him. Yet, he still wouldn't get up.

However, in the early part of the next morning, she was able to confront him, and I heard him tell her, *"I would never do nothing like that,"* while pretending to be crying. *"I would never touch no child, "I swear to God!"*

Generally, Mom wouldn't let me stay with just anybody, because she was very protective of the girls.

However, this day, she let me spend the night with my friend Denise. Before, we would always ask to spend the night, and she would always say "no." I believe she sent me away to get some rest and to calm my nerves.

When I returned home the next day, Mr. John had persuaded my mother that he would never try that. So, my mom said to me, *"You know, John always prayed, and true, no matter how much he abused me, he would say his prayers."* He was a praying person. I know that's odd! Anyway, she said, *"He probably was trying to make it to his room and went into your room."*

I think a part of Mom lived in denial.

The weekend was over; it was time to go to work and school. Mom would go to work first, then my stepdad would go, and then we would catch the school bus last.

This morning, after mom had left to go to work at the Nursery, where she worked outside in the cold or heat planting trees, Mr. John came into my room, and with his hand on one of my breast, he shook me to wake me up.

Scared to death, I awoke to see him standing over me; smirking. He said, *"Come in here and lock the door."*

He was not drunk this time. With tears in my eyes, I went with him, locked the door, and when I turned to him, he said, *"If you tell your Momma, I'm going to kill all of ya'll."* From that day forward, I went into a deep place of shamefacedness; I barely talked and internalized everything. At that moment, I walked into a place of silence, leaving others to believe that I was a shy or quiet person; a *silence* that was only a covering for a lot of secret pain.

Could I Get a Glimpse?

***"He heals the brokenhearted
and binds up their wounds."***

~Psalms 147:3

I would often think to myself, how could our biological father let us go through all of this? Where is he? What father would leave his kids and wife to live in such an environment? Would his presence even have made a difference? I'd cry at night after the lights would go out; longing to hear his voice or get a glimpse of what he looked like. Everyone would say, *"When you look at Anthony, you are looking at your Dad."* However, that did not satisfy my curiosity. The void in my heart remained.

The abandonment was painful.

Mom never spoke of him or told us anything about his person. She would just say, *"I believe he is in Chicago."*

As the years were beginning to pass, one of our oldest cousins came to visit. She told my mother that he had been killed. They said it looked like a murder, as his body had been discovered ground up in a garbage truck; only leaving his head.

My emotions were all over the place. I did not know how to feel... sad, depressed, or angry because for me, he had been our only hope of being rescued. I'm sure Mom wasn't sure how to feel either, but no matter how she felt, she knew not to show any emotion. Perhaps, it brought a sense of closure and peace to her life, so that she could now move on.

By me being the oldest and moving into my early teen years, I understood what was going on, and I knew that I wanted to attend his funeral. He was still under an alias name in Chicago, but I had no photos or knew anything more about him. I just wanted something to hold on to. Does my smile look like his? Is my brother's head shaped like his? Is his walk or his charisma like our Dad's?

I want my identity! I needed to see him...

Although Mom considered sending me since I was the oldest and could ride to the funeral with my cousin, for some reason, I was not allowed to go.

A few months later, our Mom gathered us together and told us that she was now going to officially marry Mr. John since she was now free to do so.

When she broke the news to Anthony and myself, I'm not sure she was ready for the reaction she got from us.

We were devastated. Crying, we begged her not to do that, as we were so afraid of him and hoped to one day escape all of this.

THE LIONESS

Our younger siblings were too young to understand the consequence of their getting married, as we had always lived as a family anyway. However, I could see that they had begun to become fearful; especially our baby sister, who now had a nervous condition.

We tried to talk Mom out of it, but she wasn't hearing it. She got dressed, and then she and Mr. John went to a cousin's house, where the Reverend (a friend of the family) married them. We did not even go to see this happen, and if I'm correct, he got drunk the night of the wedding and jumped on her.

I don't know what ticked him off. But, he picked her up above his head and body-slammed her on the kitchen floor; causing internal bleeding. At one point, she had to have surgery and could no longer give birth to children. I am not sure if it was from her injury or not, but I would always try to eavesdrop at the door of the bedroom to make sure he wasn't hurting her.

After she had come home from the hospital, I overheard him telling her, *"You ain't nothing. You ain't even a woman no more! Nobody would ever have you."*

I know right about now, this book may appear to be non-fiction to you. But, this was our reality!

I began to believe that things would never change; always afraid of what the end might be. In Sunday school, I was learning that everything bad that happened was the devil! Why, of all the people in our surrounding community... why us? Why does this devil appear to be knocking on our door in such a rage?

In my immature state of mind, and from being taught the 'letter' of the Word of God, I figured that we are either blessed or cursed. It seemed as though we were cursed; only living to survive or surviving to live. Our bad days outweighed our good days.

Would death be our final state?

The abuse was ever-present. Our mom was such an angel; always working hard to make sure we had our needs met. We might not have had everything we wanted, but we certainly had what was needed and a lot of love. She always wanted more for us, so in the midst of it all, we would get some of the latest things that came out... over time. After all, she was supporting five kids, a home, and if he purchased something, she had to pay for that as well.

In those days, we had to pump water, and carry it in plastic jugs. I know today's millennials would not have survived. We had the first electric pump and the first color television. Others would come by to watch the ball games and wrestling with Mr. John, and even though he did not buy much of what we had, he took credit and ownership for everything Mom did.

We had a car, which not many of our neighbors or relatives did, so they would call down the street, or send someone through that little path in the woods, and my mom would drive them to the store.

It's funny, now that I think about it. They would go to the only grocery store in town and stay for hours. You would think they had been to the Mall of America.

On the positive side, life in the country was some of the best living. It was beautiful; enjoying the summer breeze, running, playing games or sports, and eating fresh fruits and vegetables from the garden.

THE LIONESS

While growing up under pressure, my momentary escapes were when we had school functions or when we would go on church trips, where our Pastors had to preach. Still, during these visits to other churches, I would wonder what was happening or going to happen, when I got back home. Peace was far from me, and these trips were only a temporary relief. As they say, *your body is here with me, but your mind is on the other side of town.*

I was always worried about my mom and siblings; trying to protect them. Mom always said, *"If something ever happens to me, make sure your brothers and sisters were okay."*

As I aged and started to mature physically, my fear of my stepfather grew. I just never knew when something would happen to me; there was such a perverted spirit upon him. The whiskey, temper, and unclean magazines did not mix well together. And, since I was not his biological daughter, his mindset was that since I wasn't blood, then I was not "kin" for real.

Truth be told, there was a lot of incest in the community already, and Mom did her best to cover us from that environment as much as possible.

***

There was a house for sale in the neighborhood, and soon we were moving. It happened to be right next door to where my stepdad's cousins lived; the ones we used to run to for help. We liked that. There was more space than in the trailer, and behind the house was a baseball diamond.

On the weekend and in the summers, baseball and softball teams were formed to play against neighboring cities and churches. This was very exciting, and it was a great pastime for our small town.

However, it was in the back of *our* house. Therefore, we never knew what tone this would bring to our family. Sometimes Mr. John would play with them, which was pretty exciting because he was a strong man, and when he hit the ball, most of the time he'd knock it out the park! He was quite an athletic, and I heard that he had been an awesome athlete before quitting middle school to help support his mother and sisters when his father died.

Perhaps this was the source of his anger and rage. There's a reason why everybody acts a certain way.

At any rate, sometimes the ball games would end with people leaving due to fights breaking out, and Mr. John would be in the midst of it all.

I was taught in Sunday school that only God knows the future; that He is the ready writer in our life, that He holds the pen, and what He writes today will work out for our good. I remember nights lying in my bedroom, just talking to the Lord, putting what I had learned about Him to the test and praying, *"Lord, please don't let nothing happen to us or my Mom tonight. He's drunk. I hear his truck coming, so let him fall asleep in the truck."*

There were even moments I would smell alcoholic breath coming in through my window when taking a bath. I would see a shadow. He was at my window; peeping in. Fear always gripped my very core, and if I let Mom know what he was doing, she could get hurt.

THE LIONESS

Because of this, I started dressing and taking baths in the dark, since I never knew if he was watching. One day, my eyes caught some holes in the wall. Thinking that perhaps I was seeing things, I hurriedly left the restroom, just in time to see him walking out of our bedroom with that perverted smirk on his face.

He had cut holes in the wall, through the back of our closet, which connected to the restroom.

I became paranoid! When I would go to other people houses, and in public restrooms, I'd find myself looking around; thinking I was being watched or people were taking videos of me. Then, I'd rush to do what I had to do.

Either Mom or our stepdad had this big stuffed Teddy Bear; perhaps they had won it at the fair? I don't know. Nevertheless, I began sleeping with it behind me, as if the bear could protect me. It also shielded me from the views that would come through the window. I guess, as I think back on it, the bear served my longing to be covered.

One of my greatest fears, the thing I feared the most, was that he would eventually take advantage of me. I understood that God knew how much we could bear, but I also knew that this was something I would not be able to handle; my life would be over.

So, it was then that I begin planning my death. If Mr. John were ever successful in his attempt, I would kill myself. I believe this was the day that I invited the spirit of suicide that would follow me into my adulthood.

Living in Silence

"Nothing in all creation is hidden from God's sight...."

~Hebrews 4:13

This secret was kept between the devil and me; hidden in that place of silence and solitude.

My friends were intimidated by Mr. John, and he made sure that he intimated them. All of the guys were scared of him; so of course, I had very few so-called boyfriends. In some instances, this was to my advantage. Like the time I was catching the bus, and this Caucasian man began to stalk me. I told it, and he found that guy; telling him (in his choice words and threats) to leave me alone. Obviously, this guy did not know who I really was.

Or, when I got ready to go off to college, and he paid for my school clothes. I think there was a part of him that was beginning to see me in a different light.

I had begun to grow in the knowledge of God and was gifted in some areas. God would show me things that would happen before they would happen, and I would tell them my dreams and visions. To them, prophecy was a little spooky. Still, if something were going to happen, the Lord would always let me know because my nervous condition was so bad, that if it happened and I was unprepared, I wouldn't be able to handle it.

So, I did a 'Joseph' and told them my dream.

Many nights, when my stepdad got ready to act up or that demonic spirit would come over him, and he would go into a rage, I would open the Bible. Even drunk, he was a little fearful of this and would tell me, *"Get that thing away from me!"* often this was enough to keep him from jumping on Mom.

The other thing about him was that no matter how much he had been drinking, or whatever he had done to us, he would always get on his knees and pray. Many nights, he would come in drunk and fall asleep on his knees praying. I never could understand that. But, it showed that there was a part of him that had some type of knowledge of God. Perhaps, he did not want to be or do what he was doing. Maybe this was the only vent, or place to cry for help, that he thought he had.

I'm reminded of Paul in Romans, chapter 7, *"When I desired to do good, evil is always present with me.*

Only he and God knew the truth.

THE LIONESS

Unfortunately, the physical and mental abuse continued. I just don't know how we were making it. How, with so many near-death experiences, my mom remained a strong little woman.

This particular night would be a challenge on another level, and only God had my fate in his hand. We were all at home, and as usual, he would arrive intoxicated; his eyes as red as ever. Of course, everyone was nervous and on pins and needles; even the younger kids. I don't quite remember what ticked him off. Maybe there wasn't enough food in the house and mom had nothing to cook, or he had an evil thought, but he was about to hurt Mom.

We began crying and begging for him to stop when he went to his room to get his gun. This gave us a little time to leave the house and hide. We were all running in different directions... How pitiful!

Well, I ran down the street to run to the neighbors, and as I was running, I hollered, "I hate you and how you are treating us!" This took his focus off of looking for Mom; instead, turning all of his attention on me.

He immediately came after me and started calling me all kinds of two and three letter words. I ran right past the neighbor's house and hid in the back of one of their trailers. He was outside talking about, *"All I have did for ya'll and you going to say that!"*

In that instance, I decided to come out from behind the trailer, because I knew that I was putting other's lives in danger. I realized that it could be possible that it was my time to die.

Nervous and crying, I came out to face him.

Somehow, he turned the gun on himself and pulled the trigger. Jesus! He shot himself right in front of me!

Standing over him, I was hysterical and begging him not to die. My mom came out of hiding, and when the ambulance arrived, she rode with him to the hospital.

This was traumatic!

I could not rest; if he died, I would be tormented.

As I think back over this episode, I did not hate *him*; I hated his ways! I don't even know how to hate anyone; no matter what they did to me. Hatred was nowhere near my heart. As Mom always taught us, forgive quickly.

Thankfully, he survived the gunshot, and the five of us children went to visit him in the hospital a few days later. Teary-eyed, I hugged him; glad he was alive.

I was never sure if he really remembered the details of the event since he was so intoxicated that night, and as our family did not talk much about what happens in our lives, we just stayed in that place of shame; just tucking it away under layers of silence in that vault of trauma... that place in the soul where our emotions try to find peace and rest.

※ ※ ※

My best friend was my brother Anthony, and we had so many secrets between us. The only person, if I talked about anything, would be to him.

Anthony and Mr. John's relationship was now beginning to be kind of bittersweet. He had taught Anthony many things, like hunting and fishing, and he was a great example of a hard worker.

However, my brother was growing up, and things were beginning to change. He always would say, *"I am supposed to protect since I'm the next man of the house."* Plus, we were getting tired of running and hiding from the gunshots, tired of the abuse, anger, and bitterness had begun to sit in us; even the more with Anthony.

If you let it, your trials will shape you. Some people call it 'being a victim of your environment.' A man of God once said, *"Ninety percent of who you are is what you have gone through."* On the one hand, I hear, "hurt people hurt other people," yet, on the other hand, I realize that there are people who are extremely sensitive to another person's hurt; never wanting others to go through what they went through.

Let's pause for a minute... When domestic violence is in the family, there is more damage than what appears on the outside. In everything, there is a spirit attached to it, both upon the victim and the children; rocking and shaping their world with fear, torment, insecurities, anger, and so on.

At this point, I am in my late teenage years, and we went to church one night. There was a young family that visited our church on this particular Sunday. Their father was a preacher who was raising five children by himself, as his wife had died earlier.

To make a long story short, one of his sons was a fine, bow-legged, handsome guy; complete with dimples and a beautiful smile. He was a gentleman, and he would come to visit me often.

Louis was not like the other guys. No matter how my stepdad would try to intimidate and run him off, it would not work. I remember one day, we were standing under the carport and Mr. John shot out the window, trying to put fear in him.

It still didn't work!

Even his family advised him to leave this relationship alone, and I could not blame them for feeling that way, but he hung in there. He would get mad at what he witnessed of what we were going through... but he stayed.

We began to date, and one year passed, two years passed, and we continued to grow closer together.

And, guess what? Yes, we kept it Holy!

Now, this doesn't mean that within those years there wasn't any temptation. Yet, by the grace of God...

At this time, Louis and I were unsaved, but he and his family loved them some church. It seemed like most of our dates would be going to church. And, they would come home from church to play church, where Louis would be the preacher, and they would be the congregation. They would laugh and mimic how people would shout and praise God. They did this with so much joy. With me, I was always the serious one; there was nothing to smile about, yet.

I was so broken, timid and damaged on the inside. The silence had made me so internally focused, shy, and reticent. Prior to this relationship with Louis, there had been no safe place. But, this guy was so different from the others that I wanted to be free to smile or talk without fear.

One of my favorite Evangelists, Reverend Ray, was in a revival at our church, and on this particular night, as he was preaching, the Spirit of God fell on me. I had an encounter with the Jesus that I had always read about. For the first time, I knew and felt that I was not alone. He comforted me; I hoped in Him.

I prayed unceasingly for my family. Still shy, I did not trust people. I kept a diary and wrote letters to the Lord. Whatever was on my mind would be in that diary. It was my outlet, and I could trust Him with all of my troubles.

Above all, I wanted my younger siblings to experience what I had. However, the truth is that it was not so easy living saved. I began to get picked at and was talked about for this as well. Eventually, I (and most of the other kids in the neighborhood), would backslide.

Half the preachers in the neighborhood were terrible examples. They preached, but cursed, smoked, slept around, etc. Sometimes you would hug them and come away thinking that you had just been molested.

Now, by no means, was, or is that an excuse. Everyone is charged to work out his own soul salvation. I just did not cultivate or build an intimate relationship with God.

I watched their lifestyles and allowed this to trick my mind; thinking that if this was salvation, I didn't want it. It appeared like the more I prayed, the worse things got. So, I would soon drift away; finding myself in a backslidden condition. I would often hear, within my spirit, a voice that would say, *"I'm married to the backslider."*

It seemed to haunt me.

In the midst of all that, even as a backslider, whenever I would see that spirit within my stepfather get ready to show out, I would open the Bible and start reading it.

Not long after, I was playing softball with one of the local teams. It was a great day, and we were so excited and happy. After our family came home from the game, we went into the house and found it had been trashed. Mr. John had snatched the entire wood burning heater off the wall and turned the furniture over.

Why?

Because Mom had not cooked.

If I remember correctly, he tore up the stove as well. He was gone, but we were as scared as ever because he could show up at any time, and we did not know what would happen next. So, my mom grabbed a few things from the house, and we all got back into the car and left; taking backroads and hoping that we did not meet him on the way out.

We ended up staying with our mom's brother until she could figure things out. I think she had now gained a little strength to try again to escape his wrath.

Although I still did not understand the things we were going through, I did know God was with us. Hebrews 13:5 had now come alive for me, *"He will never leave you nor forsake you!"*

Devasted, But Not Destroyed!

"The thing I feared the most, came upon me."

~Job 3:25

For every action, there is a reaction.

It was now the summer following my graduation from high school. Jr., the baby boy, began to miss his dad and felt that he needed to go back and live with him. He was the one who had spent the most time with Mr. John; sharing many intimate moments together. Like us, he also had a story of rejection and abandonment, and only he and God knew his story.

Something happened to him as well that left much anger. I understood that to a certain point Jr. knew Mr. John in a way we did not. However, Mom did not want the kids separated, and was afraid that if she left Jr. with him, he would follow in his father's footsteps, so together, we all went back.

As always, he was apologetic, and things calmed down for a while. He even tried to stop drinking, but his demon of alcohol and external pressure from the neighborhood guys always won out.

During this year, there would be many life-changing events about to prompt even greater changes.

And life, as I knew it, would be altered forever.

Mr. John got me a position working at his place of employment; which was an industrial job. It was the biggest employer in our area, and paid well; however, I found out quickly that this job was not for me.

We were making plywood used for building houses. I had cuts everywhere and splinters in secret places. But, yes, the money was good.

I worked there during the summer, and then I went off to community college. As a bookworm, I continually craved knowledge, and let my brother tell it, if it wasn't in a book, I would not get it. I loved school and wanted several degrees, a briefcase, and a career in corporate America.

Above all else, I wanted to make my mother proud of me; especially since she had struggled so hard making sure that we had everything we needed. My dream was to help her take care of my siblings; to take her off her job, so that she did not have to work so hard. And, of course, to be an example for my siblings.

Someone once said, *"If you want to make God laugh, tell Him your plans."* Well, at least, I gave Him something to work with.

Also, during this year, Louis told me that he had accepted Christ in His life and was called to preach. Now, might I remind you that I was still in a backslidden state? Nevertheless, I was happy for him.

It did motivate me to want to get my life together, but I had to want that for real and not because of him. I loved this guy, and I could tell his whole life had changed; he even looked different... there was such a glow on him and a greater tenacity for God.

We continued dating, and one night he came to see me at Momma Mae's. It was one of those nights that we had to go to her house for safety, and on this particular night, he said, *"I love you, but I'm going to have to break up with you."*

I cried, thinking that perhaps, my chaotic life had finally become too much for him. Even though he said it wasn't that, I did not believe it. And, although it was painful, I respected the fact that he had come to me as a gentleman to let me know. Going back into the house, already shaken up and nervous from the episode that had occurred earlier, I told my mom, and she cried with me; apologizing for the life we were living.

Inside, I was torn-up and began to give in to the voices of others; including one lady who met my mom in the store and told her that I didn't deserve a decent guy. There was so much pain, but I had to honor Louis' words.

To make a long story short, three months afterward, we got back together. I was to find out later that he did not leave because of what our family was going through, it was because he had gone back to dating an old girlfriend and wanted to see which one of us God wanted him to one day plan a future with and perhaps marry.

We were both around seventeen years old at this time, and we discussed the possibility of me relocating to a college on the coast near him.

I did not see any way of that happening.

Who would take care of and cover my younger brothers and sisters? I couldn't put that burden on Anthony. Although I was a little angry with Mom, as I did not know why she continued to stay, I had promised that I would never leave her. Even during times when we were joking around, I would tell her that if I ever got married, I was going to have to move my husband in with her.

I was such a momma's girl; our traumatic experience gave us an unshakeable bond. I tell you, if she got hurt or something happened to her, I already felt that in my spirit. No matter what, I would feel her pain at the exact time that it happened to her. We would cry together, and I would tell her, *"Mom, it's going to be alright."*

So, after some time, I spoke with her about it, and she basically told me *indeed!* I was grown now, and I had to find my way and live my own life.

She told me that I could not live her life for her.

Not long after that, I had come home from classes at the community college, and it was as if a spirit had gotten on me... to relocate immediately. It felt like an out-of-body experience. I could see myself adhering to the call and making steps towards going off to college. Still, the part of me that was concerned about my family and their state was warring on the inside.

Who... me? I had to stay to suffer with my siblings and help my Mom! I was in the middle of a semester; nevertheless, I went to the Gulf Coast and applied to another college. I thought, *if this is God, everything will work out. He will take care of my family.*

Then, I called my best friend from high school, who was already located there and found a place to live. The college accepted me, I did not lose any credits, and overall, it was a smooth transition.

I can still vividly remember the day I packed my car to move to the coast; with Mom helping me. The memory brings tears even now. I went to hug her goodbye, and she said, *"Just go ahead on and go, so you can get off the road,"* as I looked at her through my rearview window. As I drove away, I could see her with her head down, trying to fight away the tears.

My heart wanted to turn back, but my foot stayed on the gas, and I believed I cried all the way to the coast.

* * *

I would call home daily, as the weekdays were calmer; just every now and then something would pop off. On the weekends, as soon as I got out of my last class, I headed home to be there with them. I did not miss a weekend.

Each night, after I got home from school and after the lights went out, I would get into bed and cry myself to sleep. I constantly wondered if they were okay. How could I go off and leave my mom and siblings in that condition?

Two weeks after I had left home for college, I came home from classes, and while sitting on the couch reading my Bible (even though I was a backslider, I still read my bible), a great fear came over me.

I felt my Mom.

In a vision, I saw a gunshot, and it looked like my stepdad had shot my Mom. I thought I was losing my mind. I couldn't tell if it was really happening or if that the thing I feared most had gotten into my head. Perhaps, this was only nervous energy.

Well, the home where I lived did not have a telephone, so I went across the street to a neighbor's house to call home; to hear my mother's voice and to make sure that it wasn't just my imagination running away with me.

When I knocked on the door, no one was at home. So, I continued to wrestle with my thoughts... this couldn't be happening. In my mind, I was screaming and talking to the Lord, *protect my family*. Going back to the house where my friend was, I chose not to say anything; though I struggled with how I was feeling.

Later that night, I had taken a shower and was sitting on the couch, rolling my hair, and watching television with my girlfriend, Denise, and there was a knock on the door. Her cousin came in and said, *"Donna, we got a call from your cousin, Shirley, and she said that your mother has been shot. It doesn't look good."*

My God! I couldn't even scream. All, I could think of was to get to my siblings, my mother had told me from a child, if something ever happens to me, you make sure your brothers and sisters are ok. Denise did not go with me, and I did not blame her; this was too deep, even for me, to handle. So, I told them that I would get my boyfriend, Louis, to ride me, and with my younger brothers and sisters in mind, I left to drive the 20 miles to his house.

Upon arrival, I met Louis' dad at the door and told him what had happened and that I wanted him to drive me there. He said, *"Louis, his sisters, and his brothers, have gone to church somewhere and I'm not sure where they are, or when they will be getting back."*

This was so bizarre because I always knew where he was, yet this time, when I needed him the most, he was not there. I'm also sure his father did not want him involved either.

I could not wait any longer, as my mom's voice continued to ring in my head, *"Make sure your brothers and sisters are okay if something ever happens to me."* Not knowing my mother's condition, it was now left for me to make the hour and a half drive home... alone.

Louis' father said that he would tell Louis about everything and that he would keep my family in prayer.

It was past midnight, and I was driving as fast as I could; eighty, ninety, a hundred miles an hour; all while crying, screaming, and pleading with the Lord to save my Mom. I was running red lights and all.

Then, I saw police lights behind me. However, when I began to pull over, they rode right on by, as if they could not even see me. It was as if I was invisible! With all that is within me, I felt all alone and comfortless. Still, as I look back, I do believe that night, Jesus took the wheel!

I began to plead with God.

"Father, if you would save my mom this time, I will serve you for the rest of my life! Please, Father! Help us! Save my Mother, Jesus! Don't let her die!

Upon giving my vow, there was such a peace and a presence that came over me in that car. It was the Father. My Comforter! He arrested my spirit.

And, I was able to drive home.

He Assured Me

*"Peace I leave with you, my peace
I give unto you: not as the world gives,
give I unto you. Let not your heart be troubled, neither
let it be afraid."*

~John 14:27

Driving through the night, I made it to grandfather's house, hoping my siblings were there and safe, but they were with Mr. John's sister.

The Lord had assured me that all was well, so I was resting in Him. After getting some sleep, I would awake, go and check on my siblings, and then afterward I drove to the hospital to see Mom. To my pleasant surprise, by the time I had arrived, I discovered that Louis had beat me there.

The doctors said, *"The bullet was a hair-length from her heart. We could not remove it."* Nevertheless, I had a blessed assurance that all was well and that the Doctor, the One who had never lost a patient, had visited me. It was only the hand of God that had kept her alive.

And, upon my confession!

Sometimes, the Lord will have to get you by yourself, so that He can speak or deal with you. It wasn't the will of God that someone drove with me that night. It was a time of submission, and in that place of solitude, we might talk, and I might listen.

That's the very day that I gave up my will for His will to be done in my life. A songwriter wrote a song that stated, *"I made a vow to the Lord, and I won't take it back!"* Somedays, it is a struggle to stand, but the *Vow!* Many days I felt like throwing in the towel, but the *Vow!* Sometimes, being ridiculed, timid, or fearful, but the *Vow!* Days of walking alone, but the *Vow!*

Mom was hospitalized, and in the meantime, our Dad was in jail. I thought that this would probably be an opportunity for our escape and Mom could now be free. I hated to think that way, but I just knew that if he shot somebody intentionally, it was considered attempted murder, and he would surely go to prison.

I was so angry to see Mom in that state, with a hole cut in her side, so that they could run a tube up to her lungs to drain the fluid off. From time to time, she would have a flashback of the shooting and sigh under her breath, and the tears would roll down her cheeks. I was so hurt and angry, but sympathetic as well. My heart was as tender as hers. I couldn't find any hate inside of myself... although I wanted to.

✷ ✷ ✷

THE LIONESS

A couple of days later, I went to visit my stepdad at the jail; to confront him. I stood outside to talk to him through the fence, to ask him, *why did you do this to my Mom?* Before I could open my mouth to speak, he acted as if he was so concerned about Mom's well-being, apologetic until it no longer had any meaning.

He always had two sides to him, so I wasn't sure if it was real or not. Still, my heart of compassion, only allowed me to cry and make a quick run back to the Coast. Every mile I drove, the anger was setting in on me. Then, once again, I felt the Comforter! I felt that same peace I had experienced before.

With all of this happening, I decided to quit school, but Mom begged me to continue. The guilt of not being there for her and my younger siblings was too painful. However, she encouraged me to stay on, and although my siblings were still traumatized and not in total agreement with her, she cried and pleaded with me not to quit. So, I was back and forth between school and home.

Once Mom got out of the hospital, they eventually released my Mr. John from jail. I believe at this time that Mom was working at the Police Department as a dispatcher. Somehow, she did not think he would survive prison, so she was able to get him released.

In my mind, I wanted to sue the entire state of Mississippi *and* the police. How could this happen? He had shot somebody, almost killed them, and he just gets out of jail?! This matter should have been out of her hands; but, Mom had her own thoughts and reasoning. None of which I understood.

To me, when it is a life and death situation, you need to get out as soon as God opens the door... Run!

I don't care if you think it is love. Don't let your emotions cloud your decision because they can lie to you. Emotions can say he is sorry and wants to change; however, the reality is that nobody can change a person, but them and God.

My Next Chapter

***"The steps of a good man
are ordered by the LORD:
and he delighteth in his way..."***

~Psalm 37:23

Louis and I eventually got married. Together, we planned on not having children until at least three years of marriage when I got out of college.

Didn't I say earlier that the best way to make God laugh is to tell him your plans? Well, would you believe, we went on our honeymoon and came back with Jr., then nine months later, baby Dee, and four years later, I would give birth to my third child, the Daddy's girl.

College was definitely on hold.

We began to go into ministry. I knew that he would. He had always told me he wanted to be a preacher; even when he was in the world. In our time, it was rare for a young man to preach in his teens, so we were quite busy with a new marriage, new babies, and new ministerial opportunities. We were so busy that I don't even see how we had time to make babies!

And, in the midst of it all, I was still trying to run home each weekend to check on my family; causing a strain on our marriage, at times. I would go and hang around as much as possible. At least, until I felt that they were somewhat okay.

Sometimes, I would bring them home with me, to get a break from it all and take them to my church. Each time one of them graduated, I tried to help Mom out; buying clothes, pictures, and other things graduating seniors need.

My husband was so ambitious and driven when it came to ministry. I focused on my family and made sure I was his greatest supporter and cheerleader. Mom always taught us to submit and honor the God that's in the man, that he was the head of the house. I already had a great fear of God concerning the man of God; even things that I did not agree with, I still accepted his decisions. However, the one thing in her teaching that I did not entirely agree with was he made the final decision always. I believed both of our opinions mattered and sometimes, I had the wisdom he needed.

Mothers of the church taught us to just pray about it, and you study to be quiet; don't stress him out. Make sure you replenish his strength (if you know what I mean). And, now the Pastors teach who is your mother? Who is your father? They teach us to SELL OUT! If it comes down to your family and the House of God, you give up your family before you give up God.

This passage... *"If any man come to me, and hate not his father, and mother, and wife, and children, and brothers, and sisters, yea, and his own life also, he cannot be my disciple."* (Luke 14:26)

In retrospect, the scripture means to put God first in your life, don't let anything separate you from the love of God. It was not intended to be used as a controlling factor or to manipulate your spouse as if she or the family did not matter.

According to 1 Timothy 3:5, *"For if a man know not how to rule his own house, how shall he take care of the church of God?"* This was taught so much in error that it was wrecking families.

The first church *is* your family.

So, Louis and I went into ministry-building ministry. So much so, that some days we were more like roommates than husband and wife. When you don't cover all the bases, it gives place to the devil.

In reflection, my life experience had been so traumatic that I needed time to deal with myself; to heal. But, according to the way we had been taught, this was not permitted. Your opinion and feelings did not matter; everything and everybody else came first.

And, my husband went hard on what he believed. So, each time I was in despair, I had to stay by his side and walk softly because it could cost me my marriage. This is by no means blaming my husband. I understood his desire to be all that he could be in God...

No matter what it cost.

And so, I lived my life through serving others. I loved those people to life, with all that was in me, because they were God's people. Yet, although I was leading, my issues were still lying dormant; right under the surface. I felt like *Jesus, I do not have a will. My will is to do the will of the Father and my husband.*

We eventually left our traditional churches, as my husband believed in praising God and our churches did not believe in speaking in tongues, prophesying, and dancing. My husband had another spirit being in a traditional ministry, and they were not having it; it was not in their handbook. I was more mild-mannered, walking into this newness, but I had a personal relationship with God. We just wanted more of God!

We did not leave with the wrong attitude, knowing that it had its purpose! One planted, another watered, but God got the increase. Our home churches had given us a spirit of knowledge and our beginning; we just had outgrown it, and God was calling us higher.

As the Lord ordered our steps, we joined a ministry that introduced us to the Holy Ghost! We were bold, even as young adults, casting out devils, and fasting for thirty days. In this ministry, women were to assist their spouses, and their doctrine stated that women were not to wear makeup, earrings had to be studs (if you wore jewelry), and no pants.

I remember asking my Pastor why we could not wear pants and he said, *"That's just the way it is."*

As I was very active and had come from a background in sports, and had a desire for fashion, makeup, and modeling, I did not think I could get with that. However, because we were under that covering and leadership, we submitted to our leader. My husband was the assistant pastor and co-founder of this ministry, but no matter the cost, if we had to be ugly and wear our clothing two sizes too big to receive more of God, we did that.

THE LIONESS

Though the outward man WAS perishing; the inward man was being renewed day-by-day (2 Cor. 4:16).

I was growing in the things of God. And, not being one you could just persuade to do anything, I was very submitted to my Husband. If this was where God was leading him, then *whither thou goest, I will go; and where thou lodgest, I will lodge: thy people shall be my people, and thy God my God."* (Ruth 1:16)

Let's go!

When I would go back home, my siblings and parents began to watch me rapidly go through changes. As God was introducing Himself to me, I wanted to introduce Him to them. As I look back, I think we were a little self-righteous and judgmental. They did not know what had happened to me. They knew I was pulling on God; they just did not know if I had gotten into a cult or what.

In some cases, they would be both glad to see us come *and* glad to see us go. Even though they thought we were strange, they still believed that I could get a prayer through. And of course, I tried to bring them with me; to experience God on another level. I took every chance to introduce them to God and faith in Him so that even when I was away, their faith would not fail them.

Even my stepdad was a witness to the changes. I remember when Louis and I stayed with them for a short time, and as I passed by their bedroom, Mr. John said to me, *"I am sorry for what I did to you."*

Somehow, in the midst of all that he had done, although at times I would feel anger, I couldn't hate; always tender-hearted and looking beyond the fault and seeing the need. No matter how he had treated *or mistreated* me, my stepdad was able to see

Jesus in me. When a man's ways please the Lord, he maketh even his enemies to be at peace with him. (Proverbs 16:7)

Slowly, things began to change with him. He now had fewer outbursts against Mom; however, now the children had grown both in age and stature and had begun to intervene. For the years to come, my siblings would live or adapt, without me. When things would happen, they had to act then, and I was not close enough to them to intercede on their behalf.

They each have their own testimony of survival together; having had the gun pulled on them in my absence. I would still have my moments of feeling their pain; days I would want to stop, quit, give up, and go back home to them.

Until the day I had another visitation.

This time, I was crying out to the Lord to help my family, when a quiet voice spoke to me and said, *"I am a Promise Keeper!"* Once again, a peace came over me, and I had no choice but to trust the voice of God that even in my absents, in the midst of the chaos, He had a shield of protection upon them.

I had my own issues. I was growing spiritually, even in my brokenness. I was not a radical person, but the ministry was radical. My husband had a radical praise; therefore, they accepted Louis, but they rejected me. My local church accepted me, but the sister churches did not acknowledge me as his wife, in the same way they did for the other First Ladies and Pastors.

Still, I remember (years later) the time my husband was preaching in a revival at a particular church from the organization. When we arrived, the First Lady greeted me with a beautiful corsage, although it was not a special occasion. She said to me, *"I remember when you were under our ministry, they pinned all the First Ladies and overlooked you. This is for you."*

Even when people were disrespectful or just mean, I never retaliated. I guess, what they might do to me was light compared to what had already happened to me.

Now, on another note, if you disrespected my husband (and especially my children), that would break the silence; I was very protective of my family.

There was a small community church in which an older Mother owned, a church that the Pastor had resigned from, so she called on my husband to come and help her out. They were more out front, whereas I was somewhat in the background; however, I supported them even if I was not always in agreement. He helped her for a while until he was led to start his own work.

Louis was young, zealous, and loved ministry.

We had a group of people who were on fire for God; ministering on the streets every Saturday, as well as in the jail and the Job Corp Centers… you name it.

It was all about souls and soul winning.

In the process of this, I was a young mother, working on a job, and trying to find my way back to college.

Soon, Louis felt lead to go into full-time ministry, which meant I would have to continue working. But, I was not satisfied with jobs; I always felt there was more for me as well, and if he was living his dream, I wanted to go up with him. So, a small part of me was resentful towards him for that, but I was a very submissive wife and continued to follow him.

Roaring in Anguish

"... Saying, 'Father, if you are willing, remove this cup from me. Nevertheless, not my will, but yours, be done."

~Luke 22:42

Louis decided to submit our church under an Apostolic Ministry that introduced us to the five-fold; which would later enable Him to walk into the office of an Apostle. We had a prayer room in our house, where the presence of God was very potent.

On the night of New Year's Eve, I was home with our children, and I went into prayer. The Lord spoke to me and said, *"If you make it through this trial, then I'm going to make you a Mother of Many Nations."*

We were not afraid of trials, and I thought the worst was already behind me; therefore, I was excited about what I heard, and I shared it with Louis, but his mind was in another place, I did not get the reaction from him, that I had expected.

I remember saying that my marriage was perfect. Compared to the way I came, it was indeed great. We had little to no money, and many struggles, but it was good in my eyes. I was determined not to let my kids go through what I had gone through.

So, it was well.

It seems as though when I made that statement, the devil heard it! About a week later, a trial hit me that was devastating, our marriage and our ministry were touched.

My husband would tell me later that he had an affair.

The effect of this trial had a completely different impact than the trial I had gone through in my childhood.

It woke up every spirit that was lying dormant in me; all the anger, hurt, insecurities, and especially the spirit of suicide, manifested. I could not believe the Lord was allowing me to go through this. I had given every fiber of my being for the cause of Christ. I thought I was safe. The sting of this trial did not put me in remembrance of what God had spoken to me in my quiet time.

Somehow, I was internalizing everything someone did, or I thought they had done to me. I was committing spiritual suicide, and with my self-esteem so low, I accepted every word I was called. I had always been rejected and talked about, so *perhaps I am what they are calling me,* I thought.

Then, I would go home, close the door of my room, and cry into my pillow so that my children would not hear me. The pill bottle in my hand, I wrestled with the spirit of suicide; the most critical battle was to make it through the night. Each time I heard the voice of one of my children that would keep me because *who would take care of my children if I died?* My husband was too busy, and how would this be explained to my mom? She had already been through so much.

I would conquer it that night, until the next night.

Louis was not used to women being emotional; he had come from a family of strong women. When I would go through, he would leave me to myself, and I would cry silently. Anytime I got too angry it would come up. When I thought I was delivered from it, it would show itself again. I just could not shake that spirit.

Each time I would try to talk to someone about it, they couldn't relate, and those I thought I was confiding in confidentially, would preach on me. Or, in those days, I was their testimony; I would hear others talk about what I had spoken in secret. So, to protect myself, I walled myself up again and continued to suffer in silence.

My oldest child said to me (he had the gift of discernment at an early age), *"Mom, when I get married, I want to marry a thug."*

"What did you say?

He replied, *"Because, if I did something to her, she would say 'be here when I get back.' At least, I had time to run."* Oh, my! What he was saying was that I was a ticking time-bomb.

That little voice provoked me to seek deliverance. I did not want anything to be passed on to my children.

The Lioness Den

"The elder unto the elect lady and her children, whom I love in the truth; and not I only, but also all they that have known the truth;"

~2 John 1:1

When I sought counsel, I was told not to tell anybody about what we had gone through. This counsel did not work for me. The biggest thing one could ever have is a secret between them and the devil because the enemy will wear you out and use what he knows against you.

My silence only ignited great anger on the inside of myself from another place, and I did not like the person I was becoming. See, this spirit is nothing to play with. Some days I was so angry I was scared of myself.

I was just miserable, depressed, and bitterness was beginning to set in. This was not my person, or character, as I always loved people to life. There were days I couldn't even pray. I needed to find a way to heal and resolve what I thought I had lost. On Sundays, I would come to church in spite of everything that was going on, with the hope of hearing a word from the Lord. I was not coming only to occupy a seat, but for *the life of me.*

Lord, if it be possible, let this bitter cup pass from me.

Sometimes the Prophets would prophesy; telling me how God was going to use me to heal hurting women; that this pain, would not be in vain. It would give me comfort and strength to hold on and to keep it moving.

My heart goes out to every Pastor's wife. Through my own experience and from statistics, I know the majority of them suffer in silence. I have gone into services and been ushered to the front seats, where these women were well-dressed and looking beautiful on the outside, but I could tell that many were wounded.

Who does the Pastor's wife confide in? When you scan the audience, there is no one who walks in your shoes; not even a minister's wife could fully understand. They are entirely two different roles… and shoes.

Many negate the fact that leaders are human. Not that they were not called, or anointed for the call, but we grow in grace. My grandfather said something in my youth, which sticks with me today. He said, "No matter how old you get, you will forever be learning and growing."

We go from faith to faith and glory to glory!

All of this was happening in the early stages of marriage and ministry. I was learning, growing, and being processed at the same time. I just did not know it.

You might ask, how did you lead while bleeding? We were taught, when you hit your knees put your feelings and differences to the side to be available for His people. I was used to being a sacrifice from my childhood.

There were days when I just wanted to quit! But, there was something that kept driving me back into the House of God. Additionally, my husband did not believe in us taking a break from ministry or serving. As time went on, we would live, and we would learn; however, at this time, getting a break was not an option.

If you are the Pastor's wife, and you are unable to find someone to confide in, find another Pastor's wife to talk to. I am a firm believer, that before you jump off the cliff, or lose your mind, get help. Do whatever it takes, to get yourself free. Get godly counsel or therapy, pray, fast, seek God, or go to a conference where nobody knows you, and you can be open.

A trial is when you go through something for a short-term. A tribulation could last for years. *Indeed!* My test had become a time of tribulation; it would take me years of recovery. Since then, I have learned that whether you are a leader or not, it's okay to take time to heal; to sow into yourself.

R.O.A.R.
Rejoice. Overcome. Arise. Recover.

"Arise, shine; for thy light is come, and the glory of the LORD is risen upon thee."

~Isaiah 60:1

The ministry that we were now under was a Powerful Deliverance Ministry. I had never seen a more powerful man of God in my generation. Oh, my! He was blowing the Trumpet in Zion and sounding the alarm!

All I could do was weep before the Lord!

It was such a nonjudgmental atmosphere. I remember when we walked into the church, our Apostle was preaching a message on Predestination, which means that the actions of God are fore-ordained from eternity; that whatever comes to pass is God's Master's Plan for your life, and it cannot be reversed.

As he was ministering, he read Colossians 3:3, *"For you died, and your life is now hidden with Christ in God."* When I heard this scripture, it immediately took me back to that New Year's Eve night, when the Lord spoke to me and said, *"If you make it through this trial, I will make you a Mother of Many Nations."*

Our life is hidden in Christ, in God. We were hid. How did the devil find us? God had to show him to us.

Could it be that all the hell I had gone through the devil did it? Or, did God do it? We are taught that everything detrimental that happened to us, the devil did it.

Remember, Job was minding his own business one day when the devil came knocking on his door. According to Job 1:8, "And the LORD said unto Satan, 'Have you considered My servant Job *(Louis)*, that there is none like him in the earth, a perfect and an upright man, one that feareth God, and escheweth evil? Then satan answered the LORD, and said, Doth Job *(Louis)* fear God for nought?"

To sum it up, the LORD, himself, removed the hedge from Job, to be tried by Satan. So, the devil did not have power; he was given permission to try Job. This was a turning point in my life! I was no longer walking in condemnation. It shifted me into the right path to complete healing and deliverance.

After years of serving our Apostle, Louis was released as an Apostle to launch his own vision for the *"Dominion and Power Ministry."* In those times, most pastors' wives were quiet; our ministry was unto our husbands. And, although I was married to the Pastor for years and used to praying for him from the pew, I was not vocal.

THE LIONESS

Some people, women, in particular, would take this as an opportunity to be disrespectful. I never wanted to do anything to bring shame or disrespect to the ministry, so I never retaliated or defended myself. We were taught a woman had to be careful because she could tear up a church. My femininity brought much jealousy, warfare, and insecurity. When I would sit in the services, I always kept my legs crossed and a lap sweep over them.

What they did not understand is the reason for my posture. I had been molested as a child and grew up in a perverted environment. I would buy my clothes one and two sizes too big, in an effort not to offend them. For years I would think it was me when in all actuality MOST of them were insecure in themselves.

This applied even to some of the women that came into our church as ministers because as I was growing and developing in ministry, I had no problem sitting in the pews. And though many were preaching, I had begun to discern another spirit that had gone undetected.

On this particular day, I went to my seat as usual, and I immediately started to pick up on this one minister's spirit, which seemed wrought and unwelcoming to me. She would minister often, was well-groomed, had excellent speech, and knew how to have a quality service. Since I always greeted everyone, I spoke to this minister; however, she chose to ignore me.

My husband was preaching like a crazy man, and I looked into her eyes and could instantly see a strong spirit of witchcraft and a Jezebelic spirit.

It wanted that house, and it wanted me out.

My husband could never detect the spirit because he was such an eagle, so it always left me uncovered. God would later show it to him when this spirit would come up against him in rebellion.

Later, during a prayer breakfast, I was hosting at our church, she was one of the speakers. And, because it was a woman's group function, Apostle did not come. This minister walked right past me, where all of my guests were seated and said, *"You need to shut up and sit down."*

Now you know! Something rose up on the inside that I believe was the first introduction of the Lioness! She was a Goliath, and the spirit of David rose up in me.

I rebuked her sharply and publicly, and told her, *"Don't you ever disrespect me in that manner again."* Then, I set her down and became the speaker of the hour; my first time speaking publicly.

Through the years, I watched this spirit come into our church, and eventually, she left, but the spirit would stay there. It would leave out in a blue dress and show back up in a pair of pants. I would be confronted by this spirit for many years as if this demon was assigned to me; to buffet my flesh. It celebrated what appeared to be my downfall, and it capitalized on my weakness. It watched my every move and created illusions in the atmosphere. It would get with those who were innocent and deposit its spirit into them to believe a lie and detach from the voice of leadership.

In all of this, I was exhausted and burned out from ministry. There came the point when I could not even say "Amen," or hold my head up. I was just there; I could no longer deal with the people.

Burnout is dangerous to a leader.

The devil came to Jesus after He had been fasting for forty days and forty nights and said, *"If you are the Son of God, tell this stone to become bread."* He came and tempted him in a time of weakness. (Luke 4:3)

I had a little angel who assisted me and was very careful and sensitive to me as her First Lady. She bought me a ticket to Tampa, Florida to attend *"Woman, Thou Art Loosed."* Normally, I would back out. But, I was so burnt out, I could no longer do ministry. I needed HELP!

We had to go to the service two hours early to get a seat, as I happened to be in the company of 100K women, all desperate for the Lord. Those who were First Ladies took their mantles down to receive healing, deliverance, and whatever they were standing in need of.

I did not understand how God had used this man to initiate such a move of God for women. I did not care who He used; I just knew that I could not go back the same way that I came. He would just holler *"Woman, Thou Art Loosed,* and the power of God would hit the building as thousands of women wept before the Lord.

We went to Morning Glory, and I heard this anointed woman of God preaching with so much power and authority; the room was charged, and there was such an outpouring of deliverance and restoration in the atmosphere. I had never experienced God on that level, and even in this place with multitudes of people, it was as if there wasn't anyone in the building but me and God.

I would think that every woman who had come desperate probably had a similar experience. God was everywhere, at the same time, meeting all of our needs.

She sang a song off one of her albums entitled, *"Like the Dew"* which literally destroyed yokes off of my life.

To this day, anytime I go into my prayer room, that song ushers me into prayer. That woman of God was Dr. Juanita Bynum… what an impartation and a restoration.

I would never be the same.

When I returned home, there was such a refreshing in me. Apostle said that God told him to take me out of the pew and bring me to his side in the pulpit.

He said, *"I am your covering, and you are mine."*

That's the day my ministry began.

Now, as crazy as this may seem, I know that the devil did not do it *to us*, he did it *for us*!

So, I thank God for the devil…

We were tested, proven, and tried. Marriage and Ministry collided, and I am honored and humbled that God chose me to stand by the side of such a man of God.

I wouldn't take nothing for my journey now!

The Lioness

"But I would ye should understand brethren, that the things which happened unto me fallen out rather unto the furtherance of the gospel..."

~Philippians 1:12

Who would have ever thought, that God would have a life purpose for this little country girl from Beaumont, Mississippi? That my trial, or my death, would bring life to others? I was the 'Joseph' in my family to bring them out. He had to let me go before them because there was a famine in their land.

I had to get there so they could eat. *"Man shall not live by bread alone, but by every word that proceedeth out of the mouth of God!"* (Matt. 4:4)

If they did not eat, they would die.

All of these things were shaping me for my mantle to walk beside a man of God who bears an apostolic anointing. It was never my desire to preach the gospel; many are called, but I was one who was chosen.

All of the tears, the travails, and the rejection birthed a Lioness in me. And now, I understand my assignment and calling in the earth realm. I am not confused about who I am; I have found my identity!

My administration is deliverance.

My mission is to preach the Gospel, to birth out a generation of sons and daughters, who have dealt with confusion, mental battles, suicidal thoughts, low self-esteem, molestation, depression, fear, rejection... and the list goes on. I believe God has called me to bring healing into the lives of His people. He knew I had to take my place in the Body of Christ.

Somebody preached a message once entitled, *"You cannot kill what was meant to live.* The devil thought he had killed Jesus... and then, he heard Him ROAR when He got up on that third day!

So, it was not a coincidence that each time I felt like committing suicide, I would hear the voices and cries of my natural children. It was because the Nations were calling me! They were the voices and cries of my Spiritual sons and daughters! You see, the enemy tried to silence my voice, but little did he know that all of those trials and tribulations only provoked a ROAR in me.

God kept all of His promises to me concerning my Mom and my siblings. They are fine men and women who have beautiful families; they are in church and serving God. And, although Mr. John had cancer and is now resting in peace, Mom is living and embracing four generations.

HE IS A PROMISE KEEPER!

It is my prayer that this book brings complete healing and victory to my family. And, to those of you reading these words, I pray that you might embrace my testimony so that you might have life... and that life, more abundantly.

If you have found yourself in some parts of this story, maybe experiencing traumatic pain or hardship, might I suggest to you that your course is not a curse!

God has a plan for your life; He does not waste His trials on just anyone. God uses trials to shape you into who He wants you to be. There is a purpose in your pain, and there is somebody depending on you to make it through. There is a Lioness in you, and it is time for you to *Rejoice, Overcome, Arise and Recover!*

Love You To Life,
Elect Lady Donna Beard

About the Author

Elect-Lady Donna Beard co-labors in the gospel alongside her husband, Apostle Paul Beard Sr., in which they are founders and overseers of **Dominion and Power Family Life Center International.**

She is a very sought-after Minister; operating out of the spirit of healing and deliverance. One of her greatest sayings is "I LOVE YOU TO LIFE!"

Elect-Lady has founded several outreach ministries and programs inside the ministry, with an emphasis on Women of Power Ministries and The Lioness Den.

Women of Power (WOP) is a ministry that equips, encourages, and educates women to live out their God-given purpose in the earth, as well as to invoke them to be healed, set free, and delivered. This ministry has attracted both local *and* renowned Women of God.

"The Lioness Den," is a ministry that brings restoration, healing, and deliverance to Pastor's wives.

Elect-Lady Donna Beard has been married to Apostle Paul Beard for over 30 years, and they are the proud parents of three gifted children; Paul Beard Jr. (Betty), Cordaryl Beard, and Shamaiah Beard-Hatcher (Robert).

They are also beloved grandparents...

For more information or to connect, visit:
www.wopwithelectladybeard.com

www.ingramcontent.com/pod-product-compliance
Lightning Source LLC
Chambersburg PA
CBHW072104290426
44110CB00014B/1819